# I Can Tie My Shoes

Written by Chemise Taylor

Illustrated by Alexis B. Taylor

Copyright © 2019 by My Skills Books

Published by My Skills Books

All rights reserved. No part of this publication may be reproduced, distributed, or transmitted in any form or by any means, including photocopying, recording, or other electronic or mechanical methods, without the prior written permission of the publisher, except in the case of brief quotations embodied in critical reviews and certain other noncommercial uses permitted by copyright law.

First Printing, 2019.

ISBN: 978-1-951573-08-9

www.myskillsbooks.com

I'm ready to leave, but I am missing one thing. What do I need?

I got it! I need my shoes!

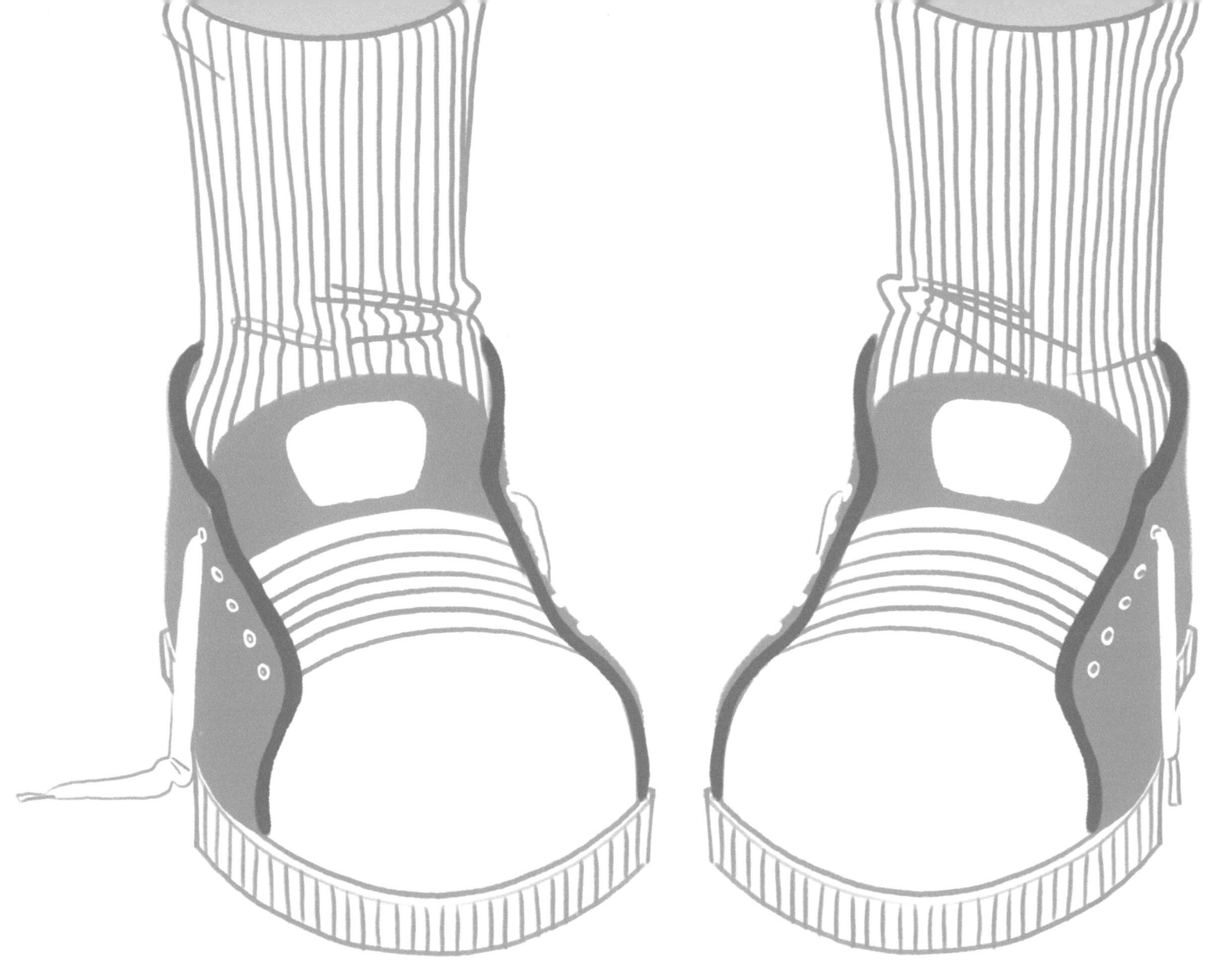

# Hmm.....My shoes are on my feet. What do I need to do next?

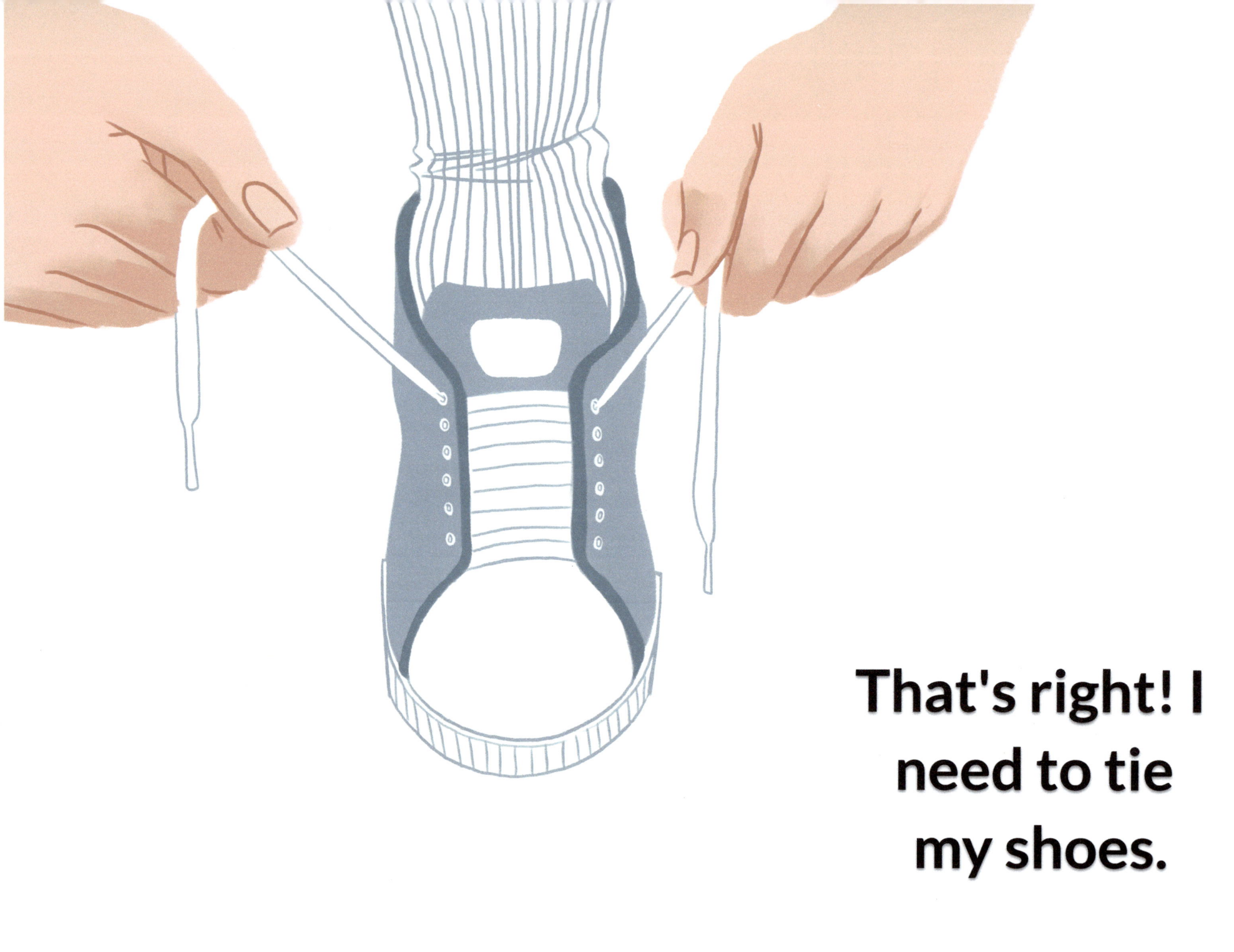

That's right! I need to tie my shoes.

I'll pick up my shoelaces and crisscross them to make a 'X'.

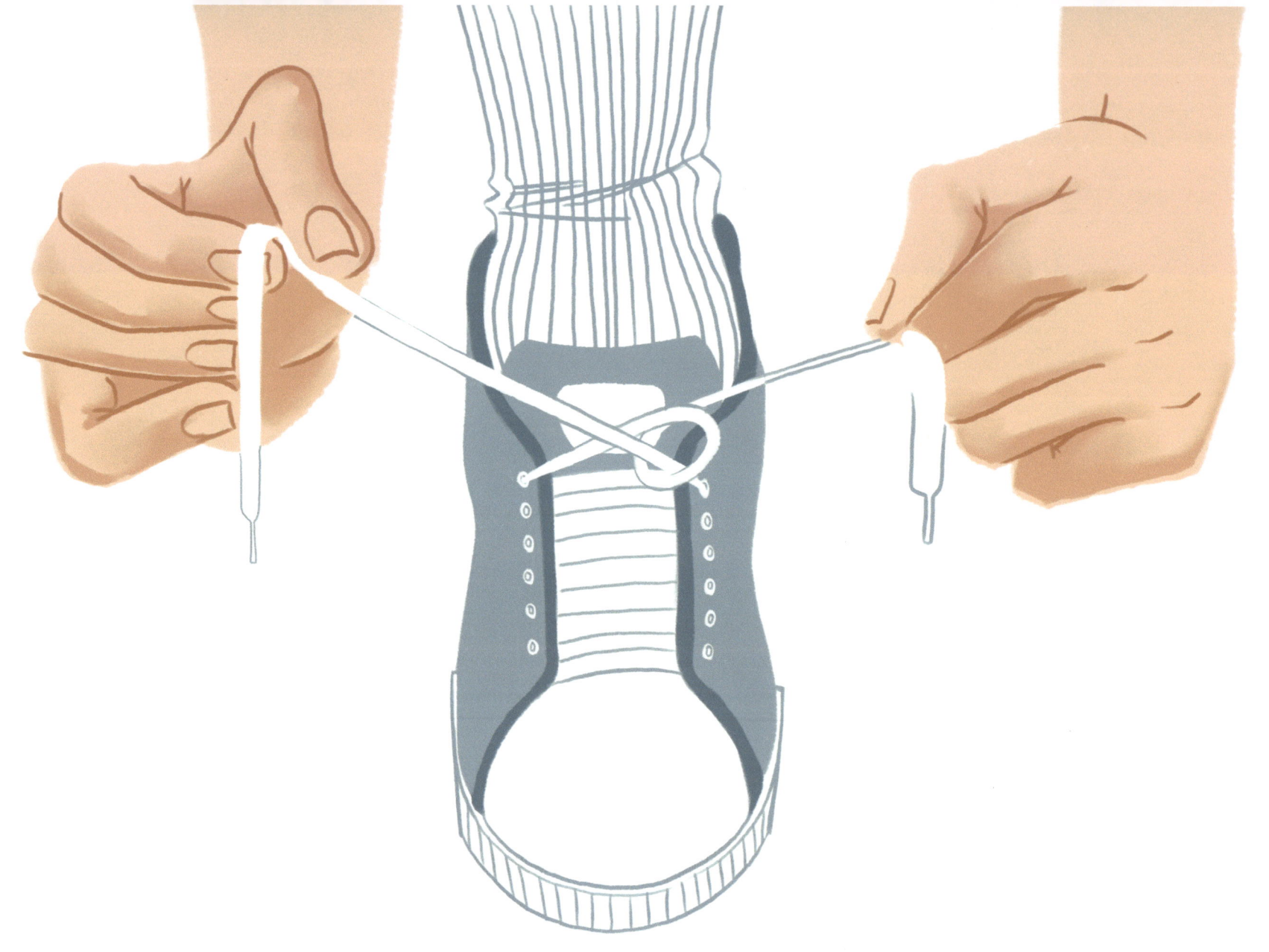

**I pull one of my shoelaces through the 'X'.**

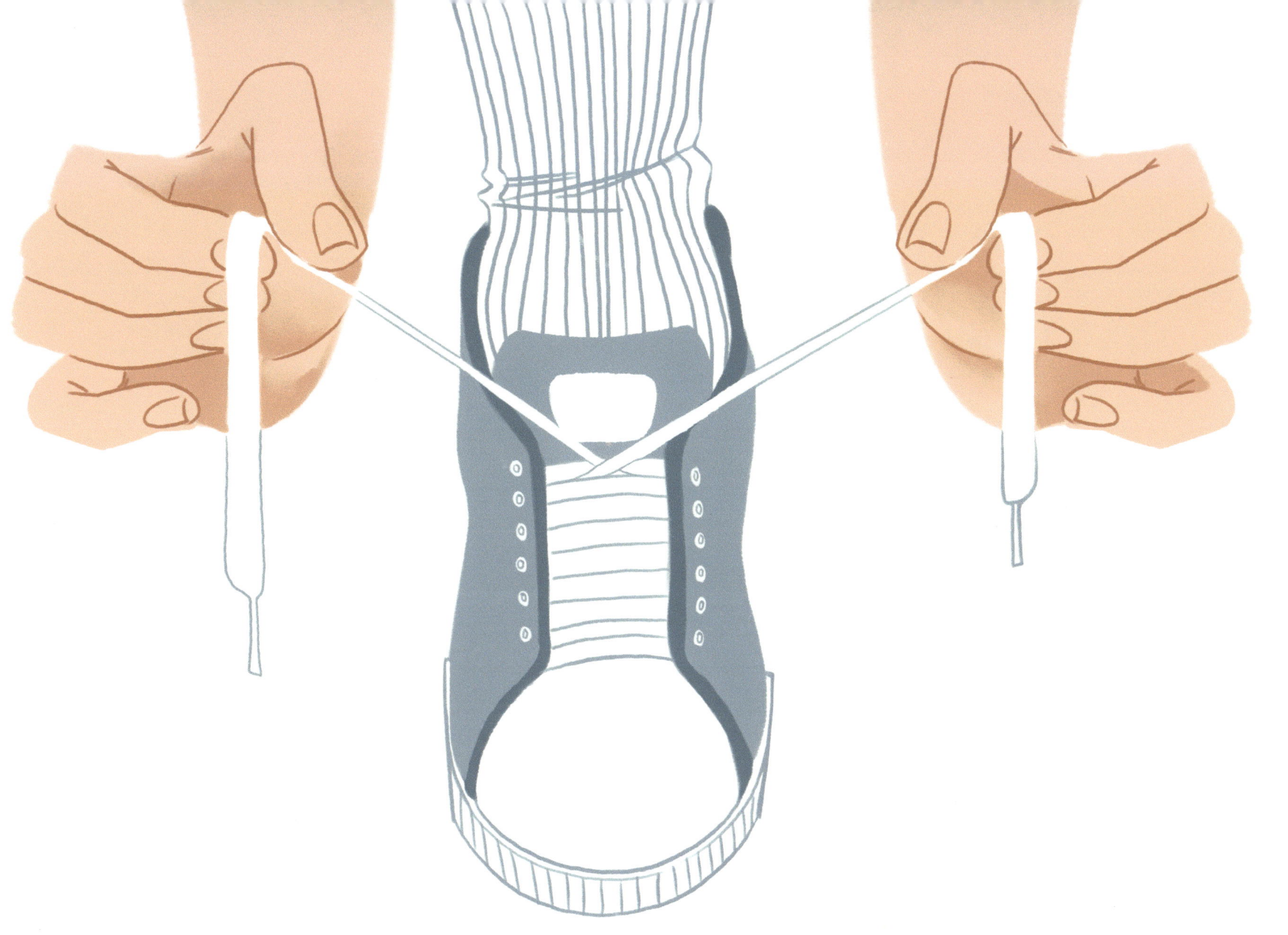

**Next, I'll pull both shoelaces in opposite direction.**

Then, I'll make a loop or "bunny ears" on both shoe laces.

Now, I'll make another 'X' by crisscrossing the shoelaces.

**Finally, I'll tuck one of the shoelaces under the 'X' and pull both shoelaces.**

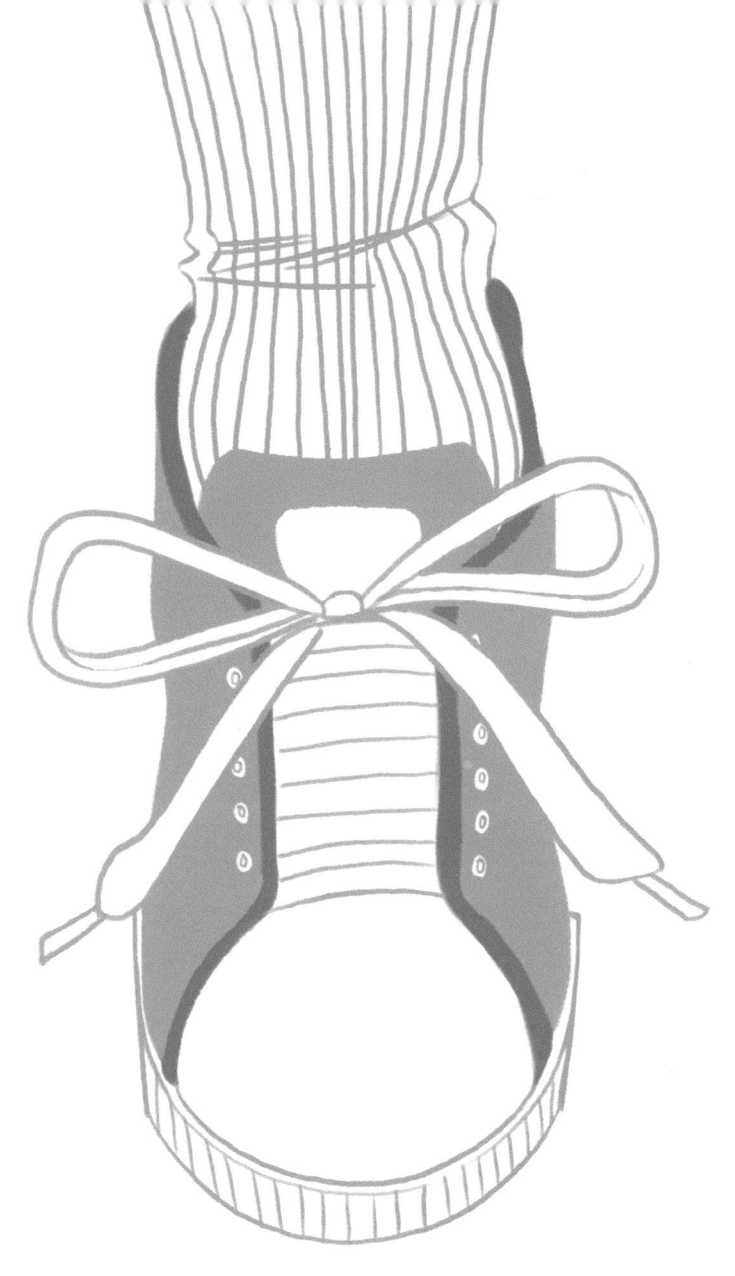

# All done! That was easy!

**Look mom, I finished tying my shoes! Let's go!**

# Book Details

**Story Word Count:** 121

**Key Words:** Tie, Shoes, Shoelaces, Feet, Loop, Pull, Cross, Bunny

## Comprehension Check

- What was the story about?
- What did he put on his feet?
- What was the name of his laces?

# Reading Award

This certificate goes to:

_____

for reading "I Can Tie My Shoes"

**Good Job!**

More books, apps and resources at myskillsbooks.com

www.ingramcontent.com/pod-product-compliance
Lightning Source LLC
Chambersburg PA
CBHW042109090526
44591CB00004B/52